This Book Belongs To:

___

___

___

INTRODUCTION

Welcome to a transformative journey designed specifically for black Christian couples seeking to strengthen their bond, deepen their faith, and manifest their dreams together. In a world filled with distractions and challenges, it can be easy to lose sight of our divine purpose as individuals and as partners. But what if there was a tool that could help you refocus your vision, align your goals with God's plan, and unleash the full potential of your relationship? Enter the "Christian Vision Board Clip Art Book for Black Couple's."

This book is not just another self-help guide or spiritual resource. It is a powerful tool crafted with love, intentionality, and the wisdom of scripture to guide you on a transformative journey of faith-filled manifestation. As a writing coach for nonfiction and a therapist, I understand the importance of blending practical strategies with spiritual principles to create lasting change in our lives and relationships. That's why I've poured my heart and expertise into crafting this unique resource specifically tailored to the needs and experiences of black Christian couple's like you.

As a seasoned expert in nonfiction writing and therapy, I've witnessed firsthand the profound impact that intentional visualization and faith-based practices can have on individuals and relationships. Now, I invite you to embark on a journey of discovery and transformation as we explore the remarkable potential of vision boards within the context of black Christian couple's lives. Through the art of visualization, guided by scripture and affirmations, you'll learn how to:

Create a vision board that reflects your shared dreams, goals, and aspirations as a couple.

Deepen your spiritual connection and alignment with God's will for your relationship.

Overcome obstacles and doubts that may be holding you back from fully embracing your divine potential.

Cultivate a mindset of gratitude, abundance, and faith that attracts blessings and miracles into your lives.

But here's the twist: This isn't just any ordinary vision board book. Within its pages, you'll find a treasure trove of vibrant clip art specifically curated to resonate with the experiences of black Christian couples. From images celebrating love, family to scriptures that speak directly to your hearts, every element of this book is designed to uplift, inspire, and empower you on your journey.

Now, you may be wondering, "But can a vision board really make a difference in our relationship?" Rest assured, I understand your skepticism. Rest assured, my friend, that this book addresses any doubts or fears you may have. With a solid foundation in biblical principles, you'll embark on this journey with confidence and conviction, knowing that God is the ultimate source of your vision and the orchestrator of your destiny

So, if you're ready to embark on a journey of faith, vision, and manifestation like never before, I invite you to dive into the pages of the "Christian Vision Board Clip Art Book for Black Couple's." Together, let's reclaim your power, align your dreams with God's will, and unleash the abundant blessings He has in store for you.

Your journey starts now.

ACKNOWLEDGMENT

Dear Beloved Readers,

As I pen these words of gratitude, my heart swells with profound appreciation for each and every one of you who has embarked on this journey with us through the pages of the Christian Vision Board Clip Art Book for Black Couple's. Your unwavering support, enthusiasm, and dedication have fueled our passion to create a resource that speaks directly to the hearts and aspirations of black Christian couples everywhere.

With every clip art, scripture, and affirmation carefully chosen and lovingly crafted, we aimed to infuse this book with the essence of our shared experiences, hopes, and dreams as a community rooted in faith and love.

Your thoughts, reviews, and experiences matter more deeply to us.

With profound appreciation and boundless joy,

Steps How to Create Vision Board

Creating a Christian Vision Board using the Clip Art Book for Black Couples is a fun and empowering process that allows you to visualize your dreams and align them with your faith. Here are some easy and simple steps to get started:

1. Gather Your Materials:
Grab your Christian Vision Board Clip Art Book for Black Couples.
Get a poster board, corkboard, or canvas as your base.
Collect scissors, glue, tape, and any other decorative materials you'd like to use.

2. Set the Mood:
Find a quiet and comfortable ambiance and play some uplifting Christian music or light a candle to create a serene atmosphere.

3. Reflect and Pray:
Take a few moments to center yourself and pray for guidance and inspiration.
Reflect on your dreams, goals, and desires as a black Christian couple.

4. Browse the Clip Art Book:
Flip through the pages of the Clip Art Book and select images, scriptures, and affirmations that resonate with your dreams and aspirations.
Look for visuals that represent love, faith, family, and any specific goals you have as a couple.

5. Arrange and Customize:
Cut out the selected clip art images and arrange them on your vision board.
Add any personal photos, quotes, or decorative elements to customize your board and make it uniquely yours.

6. Visualize and Affirm:
Visualize yourself achieving your goals and experiencing the blessings of God.
Speak affirmations or recite scriptures aloud that align with your vision and reinforce your faith.

7. Manifest with Faith:
Keep your vision board in a prominent place where you can see it daily as a reminder of your goals and the power of your faith.

8. Review and Reflect:
Take time regularly to review your vision board and reflect on your progress and growth as a black Christian couple.
Celebrate the milestones and victories, and adjust your goals as needed to stay aligned with God's will for your lives.

9. Share and Pray Together:
Share your vision board with your partner and pray together for God's continued guidance and blessings on your journey.
Support and encourage each other as you work towards manifesting your dreams as a couple.

10. Trust and Surrender:
Trust in God's timing and surrender any worries or fears about the future into His loving hands.
Have faith that He is always with you, guiding you towards a future filled with hope, love, and abundant blessings.
So, grab your materials, set your intentions, and embark on this inspiring journey together!

OUR LOVE BINDS US TOGETHER IN PERFECT UNITY, REFLECTING THE LOVE OF CHRIST.

Genesis 2:24
We are united as one in God's plan for marriage.

Ecclesiastes 4:9-10
We are stronger together, supporting each other through all trials.

LIFE IS A BEAUTIFUL ADVENTURE

WE BELONG TO EACH OTHER, CHERISHING AND HONORING OUR BOND.

Proverbs 18:22
We are blessed by God's favor in our union.

1 Corinthians 13:4-7
Our love reflects God's love - patient, kind, and enduring.

I LOVE YOU SACRIFICIALLY, JUST AS CHRIST LOVES THE CHURCH.

Genesis 1:27
We are fearfully and wonderfully made in the image of God, deserving of love, respect, and dignity.

GODFIDENCE

Proverbs 18:22
God's favor rests upon our union, and we are grateful for the goodness found in each other.

1 Corinthians 7:3
We honor and fulfill our marital duties to each other, strengthening our bond through love and commitment.

Proverbs 17:17
Our friendship is built on a love that endures through all seasons of life, providing strength and comfort in times of need.

Proverbs 18:24
In our marriage, we are more than just spouses; we are steadfast friends who remain loyal and reliable to one another.

Ecclesiastes 4:9-10
As friends and partners, we support and uplift each other through all of life's challenges and triumphs.

Friendship Goal

1 CORINTHIANS 13:4-7
WE COMMIT TO EMBODYING THE QUALITIES OF LOVE IN OUR MARRIAGE: PATIENCE, KINDNESS, HUMILITY, FORGIVENESS, TRUST, AND PERSEVERANCE.

HIS GRACE COVERS ME

Philippians 4:13
With God's strength, we can overcome any challenges in our marriage. We trust in Him to renew and strengthen our relationship.

Isaiah 43:18-19
We release the past and embrace the newness that God is bringing into our marriage. We trust Him to make a way for us, even in difficult times.

HEBREWS 13:4
WE HONOR OUR MARRIAGE AND COMMIT TO KEEPING IT PURE IN THE SIGHT OF GOD. WE STRIVE TO BE FAITHFUL AND LOYAL TO EACH OTHER IN ALL ASPECTS OF OUR RELATIONSHIP.

Psalm 92:12-14

As we grow old together, our love and commitment deepen like the roots of a sturdy tree, and we continue to bear fruit in every season of life.

Proverbs 5:18

We rejoice in the enduring love and companionship we share, reminiscing on the joys of our youth and looking forward to the blessings of our future together.

1 Corinthians 13:4–8

As we age together, our love continues to exemplify patience, kindness, and endurance, remaining a beacon of strength and hope in our lives.

Mark 11:25
We release any grievances and forgive freely, knowing that our forgiveness is intertwined with our own reception of divine forgiveness.

Romans 12:20-21
We overcome hurt and wrongdoing with acts of love and forgiveness, refusing to let evil prevail in our marriage.

1 Corinthians 13:4-5
In love, we let go of past wrongs, choosing not to keep records of grievances but instead fostering understanding and reconciliation.

Luke 17:3-4
We commit to forgiving each other readily, offering forgiveness even when it is sought repeatedly.

DREAMS

NEW HOUSE GOAL.

Life is Short, Create
FAMILY MOMENTS

My Future Family.

DREAM

Proverbs 16:3
We commit our dreams and aspirations to the Lord, trusting that He will establish and bring them to fruition.

Jeremiah 29:11
We trust in God's plans for us, knowing that He will bring our dreams to fruition, providing hope and a bright future.

PSALM 113:9
WE REJOICE IN GOD'S BLESSINGS AS HE SETTLES US INTO THE ROLE OF HAPPY PARENTS, FULFILLING OUR HEARTS' DESIRES WITH THE GIFT OF CHILDREN.

PSALM 127:3
OUR CHILDREN ARE A PRECIOUS HERITAGE AND A BEAUTIFUL REWARD FROM GOD, FILLING OUR LIVES WITH JOY AND PURPOSE.

MARK 10:14B
WE WELCOME OUR CHILDREN INTO GOD'S KINGDOM, NURTURING THEIR FAITH AND GUIDING THEM TOWARDS A LIFE FILLED WITH HIS LOVE AND GRACE.

Proverbs 22:6
We raise our children in the ways of the Lord, knowing that their upbringing will guide them throughout their lives.

Proverbs 22:6
We raise our children in the ways of the Lord, knowing that their upbringing will guide them throughout their lives.

1. Attend a Marriage Retreat.
2. Renew Your Vows.
3. Learn a New Skill Together.
4. Host a Fellowship Dinner.
5. Document Your Love Story.
6. Go on a Couples' Retreat.
7. Read the Bible Together.
8. Read and Discuss Christian Literature Together.
9. Dream and Plan for the Future.
10. Go on a Spiritual Pilgrimage.
11. Write Love Letters to Each Other.
12. Attend a Gospel Concert or Music Festival.
13. Learn a New Hobby Together.
14. Plan a Romantic Getaway.
15. Read and Discuss Christian Literature Together.
16. Create a Prayer Journal Together.
17. Plan a Worship Night at Home.
18. Volunteer together in your community.
19. Create a legacy project.
20. Celebrate milestones with a special tradition.

I AND MY FAMILY SHALL WORSHIP GOD.

Luke 14:28-30
We are diligent planners, carefully counting the cost and stewarding our finances responsibly, ensuring that we can fulfill our financial goals with God's help.

Proverbs 3:9-10
We honor the Lord with our finances, faithfully giving back to Him and trusting in His promise to abundantly bless and provide for our needs.

Proverbs 21:20
We are wise stewards of our resources, diligently saving and storing up for the future, guided by God's wisdom.

Proverbs 22:7
We are determined to break free from the bondage of debt, trusting in God's provision and guidance as we work towards financial freedom.

Soon to be mum

PSALM 127:3
WE BELIEVE THAT CHILDREN ARE A PRECIOUS GIFT FROM THE LORD, AND WE EAGERLY AWAIT THE BLESSING OF PARENTHOOD.

MATTHEW 7:7
WE ASK, SEEK, AND KNOCK IN FAITH, BELIEVING THAT GOD WILL OPEN THE DOOR TO PARENTHOOD FOR US IN HIS PERFECT TIMING.

PSALM 113:9
AFFIRMATION: "WE PRAISE THE LORD, TRUSTING THAT HE WILL SETTLE US AS HAPPY PARENTS OF CHILDREN IN HIS PERFECT TIME.

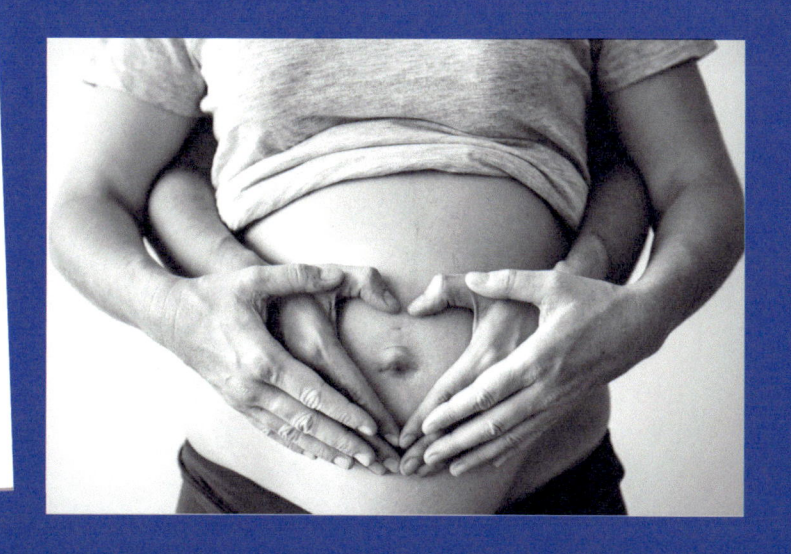

Joshua 24:15
Together, we dedicate ourselves and our family to serving the Lord faithfully, anchoring our lives in His love and guidance.

1 Thessalonians 5:16-18
We rejoice, pray, and give thanks together, knowing that it is God's will for us to live in constant communion with Him and in gratitude for His blessings.

Colossians 3:16
Together, we immerse ourselves in the Word of God, teaching and encouraging one another, and worshipping Him with grateful hearts.

20 Bible verses that inspire spiritual growth and deepen faith for couples:
1. Matthew 18:20.
2. Ecclesiastes 4:9-10
3. Philippians 2:2
4. Proverbs 27:17
5. Proverbs 31:10-11
6. 1 Peter 4:8
7. Ephesians 4:2-3
8. Colossians 3:14
9. Hebrews 10:24-25
10. Romans 12:10
11. Ephesians 5:21
12. 1 Corinthians 13:4-7
13. 1 Thessalonians 5:11
14. James 1:19
15. 1 John 4:12
16. Proverbs 18:22
17. 1 Corinthians 10:31
18. Ephesians 4:32
19. Philippians 4:13
20. Colossians 3:17

Here are 20 Bible verses about love, commitment, and unity in marriage that can inspire and strengthen Black Christian couples:
1. Ephesians 5:25
2. 1 Corinthians 13:4–7
3. Colossians 3:14
4. Genesis 2:24
5. 1 John 4:19
6. Song of Solomon 6:3
7. Proverbs 18:22
8. 1 Peter 4:8
9. Ecclesiastes 4:9–10
10. Matthew 19:6
11. Romans 12:10
12. Proverbs 31:10
13. 1 Corinthians 7:3
14. Philippians 2:2
15. 1 Corinthians 13:13
16. Proverbs 31:11–12
17. Ephesians 4:2–3
18. 1 Corinthians 16:14
19. 1 John 4:7
20. Mark 10:9

DON'T BE AFRAID

Be the Energy You Want to Attract

Financial Goals
1. Get out debts
2. Have an emergency fund
3. Find extra income
4. Have insurance
5. Plan for retirement

Be a Warrior Not a Worrier

Proverbs 31:25
As a couple, we clothe ourselves with strength and dignity, knowing that good health enables us to face the future with confidence and joy.

3 John 1:2
We pray for good health for ourselves as a couple, trusting that God desires our well-being both spiritually and physically.

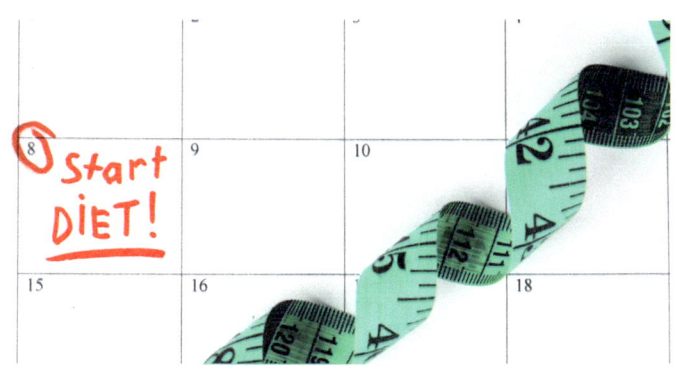

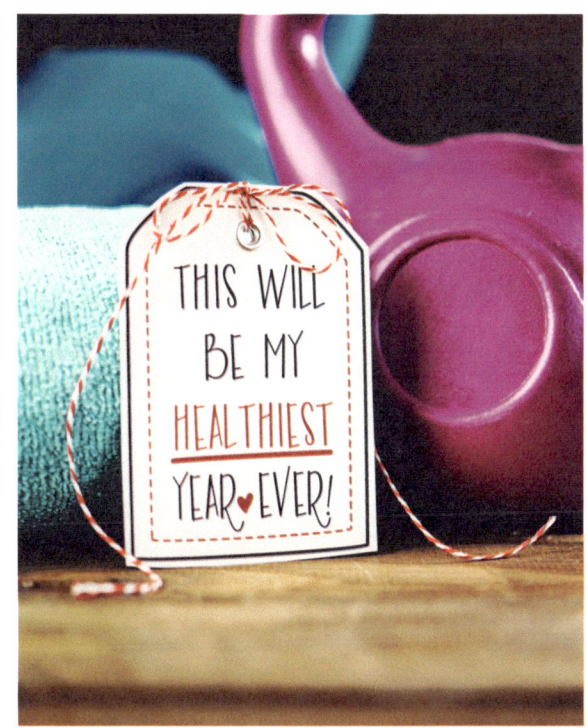

1 Corinthians 6:19-20
As a couple, we recognize that our bodies are temples of the Holy Spirit. We honor God by caring for our bodies and maintaining good health.

PSALM 106:1
We praise the Lord and give thanks for His goodness, knowing that His love endures forever in our lives.

1 THESSALONIANS 5:18
As a black couple, we give thanks in all circumstances, knowing that it is God's will for us in Christ Jesus.

PSALM 118:24
We rejoice and are glad, for the Lord has done great things for us as a black couple.

KING OF GLORY

Philippians 4:6
We present our requests to God with thanksgiving, knowing that He hears and answers our prayers as a black couple.

God Is The Plug

Pray and go to church together

~~Self-Made~~ God Made

God's Dwelling

Blessed by God, spoiled by my husband, protected by both.

Life with Jesus only gets better

Attribute Credit

1. https://www.freepik.com/free-ai-image/full-shot-romantic-couple-hiking-together_72566614.htm#page=2&query=couple&position=31&from_view=keyword&track=sph&uuid=3c079374-f7c0-4f46-b2ec-73ab9b6c37d7
2. https://www.freepik.com/free-photo/wife-receives-bouquet-flowers-from-her-husband_2753709.htm#fromView=search&page=1&position=46&uuid=ed5c014a-6bf5-4161-8684-b640b320e6ca
3. https://www.freepik.com/free-photo/front-view-smiley-couple_12406769.htm#from_view=detail_serie
4. https://www.freepik.com/free-photo/full-shot-cute-couple-posing-together-studio_49684479.htm#from_view=detail_serie
5. https://www.freepik.com/free-photo/3d-silhouette-loving-couple-against-tropical-sunset-landscape_3165915.htm#page=3&query=couple&position=3&from_view=keyword&track=sph&uuid=3c079374-f7c0-4f46-b2ec-73ab9b6c37d7
6. https://www.freepik.com/free-ai-image/medium-shot-senior-couple-nature_72566344.htm#fromView=search&page=1&position=8&uuid=b66dad16-29b5-4c22-b844-7d5a30a9139b
7. https://www.freepik.com/free-ai-image/cute-couple-spending-time-together_66190191.htm#query=couple&position=47&from_view=keyword&track=sph&uuid=3ff8a652-9c91-4638-96c7-e23e6358940d
8. https://www.freepik.com/free-photo/medium-shot-cute-couple-outdoors_39352613.htm#from_view=detail_alsolike
9. https://www.freepik.com/free-photo/family-spending-time-together-home_16275743.htm#query=happy%20home&position=3&from_view=keyword&track=ais&uuid=6a5f27ae-42fd-4480-b9b6-eeb1072ffff6
10. https://www.freepik.com/free-photo/front-view-happy-parents-kids_40287700.htm#page=2&query=family%20home&position=33&from_view=keyword&track=ais&uuid=ffb276d0-94e4-452e-987d-3a55b585b04f
11. https://www.freepik.com/free-photo/people-sharing-feelings-emotions-group-therapy-session_94668819.htm
12. https://www.freepik.com/free-ai-image/side-view-couple-getting-married_72565118.htm#fromView=search&page=1&position=48&uuid=b66dad16-29b5-4c22-b844-7d5a30a9139b
13. https://www.freepik.com/free-photo/family-three-spending-time-together-outdoors-father-s-day_38047409.htm#query=family%20outdoor&position=46&from_view=keyword&track=ais&uuid=f972edb1-1585-44e4-8c08-02be64ec89ea
14. https://www.freepik.com/free-photo/full-shot-family-members-silhouettes-outdoors_36029194.htm#query=parenting&position=4&from_view=keyword&track=sph&uuid=0d641440-8fbc-4619-96d9-1f0c752bb284
15. https://www.freepik.com/free-ai-image/young-child-with-autism-playing-with-family_138384840.htm#query=family%20playing&position=9&from_view=keyword&track=ais&uuid=8aa147b6-ffb2-4a00-a9dd-ebf22b33047b
16. https://www.freepik.com/free-photo/high-angle-modern-family-retro-style_49656730.htm#query=family%20playing&position=21&from_view=keyword&track=ais&uuid=3c5cf861-ce86-4327-9c09-84b2d05f7615
17. https://www.freepik.com/free-photo/mom-holds-legs-newborn-baby-her-hands_51398682.htm#query=newborn&position=3&from_view=keyword&track=sph&uuid=6ef24c63-bc7c-4dce-8e6a-ca02f26fe46b
18. https://www.freepik.com/free-ai-image/close-up-new-born-baby-sleeping_94954950.htm#query=newborn%20baby&position=3&from_view=keyword&track=ais&uuid=02f7bc2e-6803-45c8-bbcf-48345deebfea
19. https://www.freepik.com/free-photo/silhouette-family-having-fun-together_943136.htm#query=parenthood&position=2&from_view=keyword&track=sph&uuid=3d177ed0-fdfc-47b6-b737-81e3a2b299d5
20. https://www.freepik.com/free-photo/family-having-picnic_1165901.htm#page=10&query=family%20outdoor&position=0&from_view=keyword&track=ais&uuid=61320f48-ed3a-4699-878a-014298479467
21. https://www.freepik.com/free-photo/happy-african-american-young-family-bought-new-house_15114284.htm#query=new%20home&position=4&from_view=keyword&track=ais&uuid=e7df7851-7bbc-43e6-ac1f-f4fde9257324
22. https://www.freepik.com/free-ai-image/cute-baby-sleeping-indoors_77366278.htm#fromView=search&page=3&position=50&uuid=3ae51f32-34c3-4cb3-9f60-edfce4f427e1
23. https://www.freepik.com/free-photo/front-view-man-holding-babies_31232830.htm#fromView=search&page=1&position=42&uuid=3ae51f32-34c3-4cb3-9f60-edfce4f427e1
24. https://www.freepik.com/free-photo/full-shot-smiley-parents-with-babies_31232805.htm
25. https://www.freepik.com/free-ai-image/3d-house-model-with-modern-architecture_94952327.htm#&position=0&from_view=search&track=ais&uuid=34245f19-d881-4521-ab83-a70505fd82d0
26. https://www.freepik.com/free-photo/full-shot-couple-decorating-home_54166781.htm#fromView=search&page=2&position=3&uuid=d041f23e-95a1-410f-ae42-5ebf8816331b
27. https://www.freepik.com/free-photo/black-couple-showing-baby-ultrasound-scan-photo_2760674.htm#fromView=search&page=2&position=3&uuid=28d23d8f-5537-4933-b383-a803ad6daa17
28. https://www.freepik.com/free-photo/african-american-people-sitting-apartment-floor-after-moving-relocating-new-property-feeling-relaxed-happy-about-starting-new-beginnings-celebrating-life-event-top-view_30651728.htm#fromView=search&page=1&position=49&uuid=66b7f9c7-7172-45fb-82bd-d6ed12efcd83
29. https://www.freepik.com/free-ai-image/close-up-cople-christmas-eve_94961380.htm#fromView=search&page=2&position=52&uuid=610cc09d-1c4a-4b33-be81-8fb43a5b6383
30. https://www.freepik.com/free-ai-image/3d-rendering-house-model_66603750.htm#from_view=detail_alsolike

ATTRIBUTE CREDIT

31. https://www.freepik.com/free-ai-image/3d-car-with-vibrant-colors_66464130.htm#fromView=search&page=1&position=11&uuid=610cc09d-1c4a-4b33-be81-8fb43a5b6383

32. https://www.freepik.com/free-ai-image/concept-car-art-wallpaper_90675796.htm#fromView=search&page=1&position=17&uuid=610cc09d-1c4a-4b33-be81-8fb43a5b6383

33. https://www.freepik.com/free-photo/pregnant-woman-with-husband_2892707.htm#query=pregnant%20belly&position=23&from_view=keyword&track=ais&uuid=cca5c9d7-23a2-4dab-869a-98d86cc8aaad

34. https://www.freepik.com/free-photo/closeup-shot-bride-putting-wedding-ring-groom-s-hand_12448504.htm#fromView=search&page=1&position=52&uuid=a1e5cfa0-9f42-4f97-bf67-8e14e61286d3

35. https://www.freepik.com/free-photo/top-view-travel-items-arrangement_13358652.htm#page=5&query=trip&position=8&from_view=keyword&track=sph&uuid=76a01521-5300-4565-adc1-66d3c0accaf8

36. https://www.freepik.com/free-ai-image/couple-riding-their-bikes-beach-sunset_69840818.htm#page=6&query=trip&position=2&from_view=keyword&track=sph&uuid=76a01521-5300-4565-adc1-66d3c0accaf8

37. https://www.freepik.com/free-photo/saving-money-concept-preset-by-male-hand-putting-money-coin-stack-growing-business-arrange-coins-into-heaps-with-hands-content-about-money_14779241.htm#fromView=search&page=1&position=14&uuid=1d854ee2-5d58-4d67-a426-39f8209c59c1

38. https://www.freepik.com/free-photo/bottles-cash-with-coins-saving-money-concept_4835568.htm#fromView=search&page=1&position=36&uuid=1d854ee2-5d58-4d67-a426-39f8209c59c1

39. https://www.freepik.com/free-photo/love-letter-note-with-collection-romantic-stationery_57314038.htm#fromView=search&page=1&position=31&uuid=75c65ad3-7529-4b40-b229-f3fb22053a07

40. https://www.freepik.com/free-photo/valentines-day-guy-prepared-surprise-valentine-s-day_13181764.htm#&position=0&from_view=search&track=ais&uuid=00659c40-a551-433d-9860-a397c19483ce

41. https://www.freepik.com/free-photo/pay-off-debts-loan-money-bankruptcy-bill-credit-concept_17105778.htm#fromView=search&page=1&position=6&uuid=919f4c8f-5e55-430f-82a3-8869c63fe9fd

42. https://www.freepik.com/free-photo/list-financial-goals-table_3064062.htm#fromView=search&page=1&position=4&uuid=a4cd505e-f158-4493-b30a-4044ee797a43

43. https://www.freepik.com/free-vector/hand-drawn-body-positive-lettering_40482819.htm#fromView=search&page=1&position=14&uuid=a4cd505e-f158-4493-b30a-4044ee797a43

44. https://www.freepik.com/free-vector/retro-lettering-be-afraid_1134358.htm#fromView=search&page=2&position=40&uuid=a4cd505e-f158-4493-b30a-4044ee797a43

45. https://www.freepik.com/free-ai-image/bright-light-jesus-cross_94959956.htm#page=2&query=praying&position=2&from_view=keyword&track=sph&uuid=67cf4002-0941-4605-b1ba-edc601126f37

46. https://www.freepik.com/free-photo/motivated-active-ethnic-couple-run-up-stairs-together-jump-highly-train-climbing-staircase-city-wear-comfortable-sportsclothes-drink-water-from-bottle-climb-challenge-choose-difficult-path_12204416.htm#fromView=search&page=1&position=1&uuid=10163fbb-324f-4295-bb3b-d52850a4226e

47. https://www.freepik.com/free-ai-image/portrait-mother-with-newborn-baby_94489032.htm#fromView=search&page=3&position=1&uuid=acd57359-b0c6-4cf2-8c57-49b429c86281

48. https://www.freepik.com/free-vector/motivational-lettering-be-warrior-worrier-inspirational-quote-design_11406472.htm#fromView=search&page=3&position=2&uuid=a4cd505e-f158-4493-b30a-4044ee797a43

49. https://www.freepik.com/free-photo/travel-concept-with-baggage_19894695.htm#fromView=search&page=1&position=1&uuid=237caefb-3141-42ed-91ce-61c99ae9b369

Made in the USA
Columbia, SC
03 February 2025